This book belongs to

____

____

Aged ________

Stories For the Young Reader

THE *Castle in the Clouds*

AND OTHER STORIES

STORIES FOR THE YOUNG READER

THE *Castle in the Clouds*

AND OTHER STORIES

This is a Parragon Book
First published in 2000

Parragon
Queen Street House
4 Queen Street
Bath BA1 1HE, UK

ISBN 0-75253-419-X

Designed by Mik Martin

Printed in Spain

These stories have been previously
published by Parragon in the
Bumper Bedtime Series 1999

Contents

The Castle in the Clouds

THERE WAS ONCE a family that lived in a little house in a village at the bottom of a mountain. At the top of the mountain was a great, grey castle made of granite. The castle was always shrouded in clouds, so it was known as the castle in the clouds. From the village you could only just see the outline of its high walls and turrets. No-one in the village ever went near the castle, for it looked such a gloomy and forbidding place.

Now in this family there were seven children. One by one they went out into the world to seek their fortune, and at last it was the youngest child's turn. His name was

Sam. His only possession was a pet cat named Jess, and she was an excellent rat-catcher. Sam was most upset at the thought of leaving Jess behind when he went off to find work, but then he had an idea.

"I'll offer Jess's services at the castle in the clouds. They're bound

to need a good ratter, and I'm sure I can find work there, too," he thought.

His parents were dismayed to discover that Sam intended to seek work at the castle, but try as they might they could not change his mind. So Sam set off for the castle with Jess at his side. Soon the road started to wind up the mountainside through thick pine forests. It grew cold and misty. Rounding a bend they suddenly found themselves up against a massive, grey stone wall. They followed the curve of the wall until they came to the castle door.

Sam went up to the door and banged on it. The sound echoed

spookily. "Who goes there?" said a voicc.

Looking up, Sam saw that a window high in the wall had been thrown open and a face was eyeing him suspiciously. "I... I... I wondered if you'd be interested in employing my cat as a rat-catcher," began Sam.

The window slammed shut, but a moment later a hand beckoned him through the partly open castle door. Stepping inside, Sam and Jess found themselves face-to-face with an old man.

"Rat-catcher, did you say?" said the old man raising one eyebrow. "Very well, but she'd better do a good job or my master will punish us all!"

Sam sent Jess off to prove her worth. In the meantime Sam asked the old man, who was the castle guard, if there might be any work for him, too.

"You can help out in the kitchens. It's hard work, mind!" the guard said.

Sam was soon at work in the kitchens — and what hard work it was! He spent all day peeling vegetables, cleaning pans and scrubbing the floor. By midnight he was exhausted. He was about to find a patch of straw to make his bed, when he noticed Jess wasn't around. He set off in search of her. Down

dark passages he went, up winding staircases, looking in every corner and behind every door, but there was no sign of her. By now he was hopelessly lost and was wondering how he would ever find his way back to the kitchens, when he caught sight of Jess's green eyes shining like lanterns at the top of a rickety spiral staircase. "Here, Jess!" called Sam softly. But Jess stayed just where she was.

When he reached her, he found that she was sitting outside a door and seemed to be listening to something on the other side. Sam put his ear to the door. He could hear the sound of sobbing. He knocked gently at the door. "Who is it?" said a girl's voice.

"I'm Sam, the kitchen boy. What's the matter? Can I come in?" said Sam.

"If only you could," sobbed the voice. "I'm Princess Rose. When my father died my uncle locked me in here so that he could steal the castle. Now I fear I shall never escape!"

Sam pushed and pushed at the door, but to no avail. "Don't worry," he said, "I'll get you out of here."

Sam knew exactly what to do, for when he had been talking to the guard, he had spotted a pair of keys hanging on a nail in the rafters high above the old man's head. He had wondered at the time why anyone should put keys out of the reach of any human hand. Now he thought he knew — but first he had to get the keys himself!

Sam and Jess finally made their way back to where the keys were, only to find the guard was fast asleep in his chair right underneath them! Quick as a flash, Jess had leaped up on to the shelf behind his head. From there, she climbed higher and higher until she reached the rafters. She took the keys in her jaws and carried them gingerly down. But as she jumped from the shelf again, she knocked over a jug and sent it crashing to the floor. The guard woke with a start.

"Who goes there?" he growled. He just caught sight of the tip of

Jess's tail as she made a dash for the door.

Sam and Jess retraced their steps with the guard in hot pursuit.

"You go a different way," hissed Sam, running up the stairs to Rose's door, while the old man disappeared off after Jess. Sam put one of the keys in the lock. It fitted! He turned the key and opened the door. There stood the loveliest girl he had ever seen. The princess ran towards him, as he cried, "Quick! There's not a moment to lose." He grabbed her hand and led her out of the tower.

"Give me the keys," she said. She led him down to the castle cellars. At last they came to a tiny door. The princess put the second key in the lock and the door opened. Inside was a small cupboard, and inside that was a golden casket filled with precious jewels.

"My own casket — stolen by my uncle," cried Rose.

Grabbing the casket the pair ran

to the stables and saddled a horse. Suddenly Jess appeared with the guard still chasing him. With a mighty leap Jess landed on the back of the horse behind the princess and Sam.

"Off we go!" cried Sam.

And that was the last that any of them saw of the castle in the clouds. Sam married the princess and they all lived happily ever after.

The Dog With No Voice

THERE ONCE LIVED a prince whose words were pure poetry. He amused the court with his witty, rhyming verse, yet his kind and thoughtful words made him popular with all. It was said he could even charm the birds from the trees.

One day, he was walking in the forest when he came upon an old lady with a huge bundle on her back. "Let me help," said the prince. He took the load and walked along beside the woman. They chatted away and before long they had reached the old lady's door.

Now the old lady — who was really a witch — had been listening intently to the prince's words. "What a fine voice he has!" she thought to herself. "I would like my own son to speak like that. Then maybe he could find himself a wealthy wife and we'd be rich for ever more!"

"You must be thirsty," she said to the prince. "Let me give you something to quench your thirst to repay you for your kindness." The prince gratefully accepted, and was

given a delicious drink which he drained to the last drop. He was about to thank the witch when he began to feel very peculiar. He found he was getting smaller and smaller. He looked down at his feet and saw two hairy paws. Then he turned round and saw to his horror that he had grown a shaggy tail! He tried to shout at the witch but all that came out of his mouth was a loud bark!

The witch hugged herself for joy. "My spell worked!" she cackled. "Come here my son!" she called.

There appeared at the door a rough-looking young man. "What's going on, my dearest mother?" he said in a voice that sounded familiar to the prince. Then he looked down and exclaimed, "Where did you find this poor little dog?"

Now the prince understood what had happened. "The old lady has turned me into a humble hound and given my voice to her son. Whatever am I to do?" he thought miserably. "I can't return to the palace. They'll never let a stray dog in." He turned with his tail between his legs and trotted off forlornly into the forest.

The witch and her son were delighted with his new voice. She made him scrub himself clean from top to toe and dressed him in the prince's clothes. "Now go," she said, "and don't return until you've found a rich girl to marry!"

The young man set off, eager to try out his new voice. Soon he was feeling very pleased with himself as he talked to passers-by. "What a very polite young man!" and "What a wonderful way with words," folk cried. "He could charm the birds out of the trees," other people said.

The witch's son travelled far and wide until at last he came to a castle where he spied a fair princess sitting on her balcony. He called to her and straight away she arose and looked down into the garden, enraptured by the sound of his beautiful voice. She was enchanted by his fine words and guessed they must belong to a prince. Soon the princess and the witch's son were chatting away merrily, and to his delight when he asked her to marry him she readily agreed. "For one with so beautiful a voice," she

thought to herself, "must indeed be a fine young man."

Meanwhile, the poor dog-prince wandered in the forest, surviving as best he could by foraging for roots and fruits in the undergrowth. Feeling truly miserable, he stopped to drink from a stream. As he dipped his long dog's tongue in the cool water, he caught sight of someone sitting on a bridge. It was a pixie, fishing with a tiny net.

"Cheer up!" said the little fellow, "I saw everything that happened and I think I know how we can get your voice back. Follow me!" And with that he was off, dancing away through the forest with the dog-prince trotting along behind. They seemed to go on forever, and the dog-prince was feeling very hot, and the pads of his paws were quite sore, by the time they reached the castle. He could see the witch's son in the garden calling to the princess on the balcony.

The dog-prince's eyes filled with tears, for she was quite the loveliest girl he had ever seen and he wished he could marry her himself.

"We will be married today," the witch's son was saying in the prince's voice, "I will await you by the church, my fairest one." Seizing his fishing net, the pixie leaped high in the air. As the words 'my fairest one' floated up to the balcony, he caught them in the net and gave them back to the dog-prince.

As soon as he had swallowed the words, the dog-prince could speak again. "Thank you, little pixie," he cried, "but what can I do? Now I am a dog with a prince's voice. The princess will never marry me."

"If you want to break the witch's spell, you must go to the church — fast!" said the pixie. And with those words he disappeared.

Straight away, the dog-prince

ran to the church door. There was the princess looking most perplexed, for standing beside her was the witch's son — with not a word in his head. "I don't understand," she cried, "I thought I was to marry a silver-tongued young man, but now I find he is a dumb ragamuffin!"

"I can explain," exclaimed the dog-prince.

The princess spun around. "Who can explain?" she asked, for all she could see was a dog in front of her. "What a handsome dog!" she cried, bending down and kissing him on the nose. To her astonishment, the dog's hairy paws and shaggy tail immediately disappeared and there stood the prince. "But you're... but he..." she stammered looking from the prince to the witch's son.

Well, the prince explained everything that had happened, and after that he and the princess were married with great rejoicing. And as

for the witch's son? He wasn't a bad young man, really, so the prince taught him to speak again — with a beautiful voice — and he married the princess's younger sister.

Catswhiskers

CATSWHISKERS was a pyjama case cat, and a very fine-looking pyjama case cat at that. Susie's granny had sewn him together when Susie was only four years old. It had taken Susie's granny quite a long time to make Catswhiskers. Every night she had sat by the fire carefully cutting and sewing, until he was perfect. Catswhiskers' body was made from the finest black velvet. He had beautiful red glass eyes, a bushy tail and the longest whiskers you have ever seen. That is how he got the name Catswhiskers.

Catswhiskers sat on the end of Susie's bed, looking at all the toys in the bedroom in that slightly snooty way that cats have of looking at things.

When Susie was asleep, or playing in another room, Catswhiskers and all the toys would talk to each other. But Catswhiskers was bored with talking to the toys. Jenny the ragdoll was — well — just a ragdoll. "What could a ragdoll possibly have to say that would be of interest to a velvet pyjama case cat?" thought Catswhiskers.

Then there was Neddy the rocking horse. He was a perfectly pleasant rocking horse as far as rocking horses went, but he only ever seemed to want to talk about how nice and shiny he was, and how he thought he was Susie's favourite toy. Even the alphabet bricks, the jack-in-the-box and the brightly coloured ball seemed to have nothing to say of interest to Cats-

whiskers. He sighed and looked at the window, wondering if life was more exciting outside.

One day, he decided he'd had enough of life in the bedroom with all the toys, and that he would venture outside to see if he could meet someone more interesting to talk to. So that night, when it was dark and Susie was asleep, he crept carefully to the open bedroom window and jumped out. It was a clear, cold, moonlit night. Catswhiskers shivered a little to find it so cold outside, and he maybe shivered a little more because he was also rather frightened. But he was very excited to be in the outside world, too, and he soon forgot about the cold and his fear.

He walked along the fence to the end of Susie's garden and jumped down into the garden next door. He had no sooner landed when he heard a fierce growl and saw two big, black eyes glinting in the moonlight.

It was Barker, next door's dog — and he didn't like cats at all. With a loud bark, Barker came rushing towards Catswhiskers. His mouth was open wide and Catswhiskers could see his big, sharp teeth. In fact, he thought that he could see all the way down into Barker's stomach! Catswhiskers only just had time to leap back on to the fence as Barker, jaws still snapping, gave chase.

"Phew, what a narrow escape," gasped Catswhiskers. "I didn't realise dogs were so unfriendly!"

He was wondering where it might be safe to go next when he heard a low, hissing voice behind him. "Hey, velvet cat," hissed the voice. "What do you think you are doing on our patch?"

Catswhiskers turned round to see the biggest, meanest-looking cat he had ever set eyes on. And behind him were several more mean-looking cats, all coming slowly towards Catswhiskers with their sharp claws at the ready. Catswhiskers didn't wait a second longer. He simply ran for his life. Now he was very frightened. He was also feeling cold and hungry. He wished that he was still in the

warm safety of Susie's bedroom with the other toys. Just as he was thinking that the outside world was perhaps a bit too exciting, he heard the sound of a van approaching. It suddenly stopped, its glaring headlights shining straight at him. On the side of the van were the words STRAY CAT CATCHER.

Out of the van stepped a man carrying a big net. Catswhiskers thought he knew just who that net was for, and decided that it was definitely time to go!

Without thinking about the dangers he might find himself in if he came face to face again with gangs of sharp-clawed cats or fierce, barking dogs, he ran back towards Susie's house as fast as his velvet legs could carry him. At last he reached the window and jumped thankfully back inside.

Snuggled down again on the warm bed with all his familiar friends around him, Catswhiskers decided that perhaps this was the best life for a pyjama case cat after all.

Esmerelda the Rag Doll

AT THE BACK of the toy cupboard on a dark and dusty shelf lay Esmerelda the ragdoll. She lay on her back and stared at the shelf above, as she had done for a very long time. It seemed to Esmerelda that it was many years since she had been lifted up by Clara, her owner, and even longer since she had been out in the playroom with the other toys. Now her lovely yellow hair was all tangled and her beautiful blue dress was creased, torn and faded. Each time Clara opened the toy cupboard door, Esmerelda hoped very much that she would be chosen, but Clara always played with the newer toys at the front of the cupboard. Every time Clara put her toys back in the cupboard, Esmerelda felt herself being pushed further towards the back. It was very uncomfortable and indeed, Esmerelda might have suffocated if it wasn't for a hole at the back of the cupboard, which enabled her to breathe.

These days Esmerelda felt very lonely. Until recently a one-eyed teddy bear had been beside her on the shelf. Then one day he had fallen through the hole at the back of the cupboard and was never seen again. Esmerelda missed him dreadfully, for he had been a lovely old teddy with a gentle nature. Now she, too, could feel herself being pushed towards the hole. She felt a mixture of excitement and fright at the prospect of falling through it. Sometimes she imagined that she would land on a soft feather bed belonging to a little girl who would really love her. At other times she

thought that the hole led to a terrifying land full of monsters.

One day Esmerelda heard Clara's mother say, "Now Clara, today you must tidy up the toy cupboard and clear out all those old toys you no longer play with."

Esmerelda could see Clara's small hands reaching into the cupboard. She couldn't bear the thought of being picked up by the little girl and then discarded. "There's only one thing to do," she said to herself. She wriggled towards the hole, closed her eyes and jumped. Esmerelda felt herself falling, and then she landed with a bump on something soft.

"Watch out, my dear!" said a familiar voice from underneath her. Esmerelda opened her eyes and saw that she had landed on One-eyed Ted.

The two toys were so overjoyed to see each other again that they hugged one another. "What shall we do now?" cried Esmerelda.

"I have an idea," said Ted. "There's a rusty old toy car over there. I wanted to escape in it, but I can't drive with only one eye. What do you think? Shall we give it a go?"

"Yes, yes!" exclaimed Esmerelda, climbing into the driver's seat.

By now One-eyed Ted had found the key and was winding up

the car. "Away we go!" he called as they sped off.

"Where are we going?" shouted Esmerelda.

"To the seaside," replied Ted.

"Which way is it?" asked Esmerelda, holding on to her yellow hair streaming behind her in the wind.

"I don't know. We'll have to ask the way," said Ted.

Rounding a bend, they came across a black cat crossing the road. "Excuse me," called Ted, "could you tell us the way to the seaside?"

Now, as you know, cats hate water. "Whatever do they want to go near water for? Why should I help them?" thought the cat. "It's the other side of that mountain," he growled as he ran off.

On sped the rusty car, and up the mountainside. When they reached the top of the mountain they met a sheep. Now, as you know, sheep never listen properly. "Excuse me," said Esmerelda, "where can we find the beach?"

Well, the silly sheep thought Esmerelda was asking where they could find a peach! "Down there," she bleated, nodding towards an orchard in the valley below.

Esmerelda and Ted leaped back into the car and sped off down the mountainside, but when they

reached the orchard there was no sign of water, of course — just a lot of peach trees.

Once again they scratched their heads in puzzlement. Just then a mole popped his head out of the earth. "Excuse me," said Ted, "would you happen to know how we can find the seaside?"

Now the mole was very wise, but unfortunately he was also, as you know, very short sighted. He peered at Esmerelda's blue dress. "That patch of blue must surely be a river, and rivers run into the sea," he thought.

"Just follow that river," he said, "and you'll end up at the seaside.

Good day!" And with that he disappeared under ground again.

Esmerelda and Ted looked even more puzzled, for there was no sign of a river in the orchard. "Oh well," sighed Esmerelda, "perhaps we'll never find the seaside."

"Don't give up," said Ted. "We'll surely find it in the end." They climbed back in the rusty car and set off again. After a short while the car started to splutter and then it came to a complete halt at the side of the

road. "What shall we do now?" cried Esmerelda.

"We'll just have to wait here and see what happens," said Ted. It seemed like a very long time that they sat beside the road. At long last they heard footsteps, and then Esmerelda felt herself being picked up.

"Look — it's a dear old tatty ragdoll," said a voice. Esmerelda looked up and saw that she was being carried by a little girl.

Ted and the rusty car had been picked up by the girl's father. "We'll take them home and look after them," the man said.

Now they were in a real car

and before long the toys found themselves in a house. The little girl carried Esmerelda, One-eyed Ted and the rusty car upstairs to her bed-room and put them down on a window sill. "I'll be back soon," she whispered.

Esmerelda looked out of the window and nearly danced for joy. "Look, look Ted," she shouted. For out of the window she could see the road, and beyond the road was a beach and then the sea. "We reached the seaside after all," she cried.

Esmerelda, Ted and the rusty car lived happily in the house beside the sea. Esmerelda's hair was brushed and plaited and she was given a beautiful new dress. Ted had a new eye sewn on and could see properly again. The rusty car was painted and oiled. Most days the little girl took her new toys down to the beach to play with, and the days in the dark toy cupboard were soon forgotten. The little girl used to tell her friends the story of how she had found her three best toys lying beside the road one day. And as for the toys, well, they sometimes talked about that strange day when they had such an adventure — and they'd burst out laughing.

Little Tim and His Brother Sam

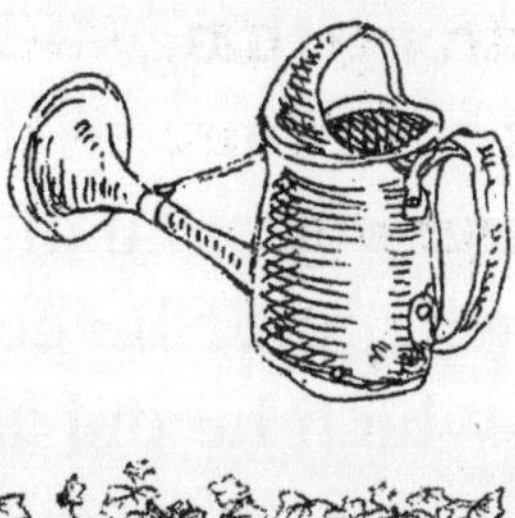

Little Tim was a very lucky boy. He had a lovely home, with the nicest parents you could hope for. He had a big garden, with a swing and a football net in it. And growing in the garden were lots of trees that you could climb and have adventures in. Little Tim even had a nice school, which he enjoyed going to every day and where he had lots of friends. In fact, almost everything in Tim's life was nice. Everything that is apart from one thing — Tim's brother Sam.

Sam was a very naughty boy. Worse still, whenever he got into mischief — which he did almost all of the time — he managed to make it look as though someone else was to blame. And that someone was usually poor Tim!

Once Sam thought that he would put salt in the sugar bowl instead of sugar. That afternoon, Sam and Tim's parents had some friends round for tea. All the guests put salt in their cups of tea, of course, thinking it was sugar. Well, being very polite they didn't like to say anything, even though their cups of tea tasted very strange indeed! When Sam and Tim's parents tasted their tea, however, they guessed immediately that someone had been playing a trick. They had to apologise to their guests and make them all fresh cups of tea. And who got the blame? Little Tim did, because Sam had sprinkled salt on Tim's bedroom floor so that their mother would think that Tim was the culprit.

Another time, Sam and Tim were playing football in the garden when Sam accidentally kicked the ball against a window and broke it. Sam immediately ran away and hid, so that when their father came out to investigate, only Tim was to be seen. So poor little Tim got the blame again.

Then there was the time when Sam and Tim's Aunt Jessica came to stay. She was a very nice lady, but she hated anything creepy-crawly, and as far as she was concerned that included frogs. So what did Sam do? Why, he went down to the garden pond and got a big, green frog to put in Aunt Jessica's handbag. When Aunt Jessica opened her handbag to get her glasses out, there staring out of the bag at her were two froggy eyes.

"Croak!" said the frog.

"Eeek!" yelled Aunt Jessica and almost jumped out of her skin.

"I told Tim not to do it," said Sam.

Tim opened his mouth and was just about to protest his innocence when his mother said, "Tim, go to your room immediately and don't come out until you are told."

Poor Tim went to his room and had to stay there until after supper. Sam thought it was very funny.

The next day, Sam decided that he would play another prank and blame it on Tim. He went to the garden shed and, one by one, took out all the garden tools. When he thought no-one was watching, he hid them all in Tim's bedroom cupboard. In went the spade, the fork, the watering can, the trowel — in fact, everything except the lawnmower. And the only reason that the lawnmower didn't go in was because it was too heavy to carry!

But this time, Sam's little prank was about to come unstuck, for Aunt

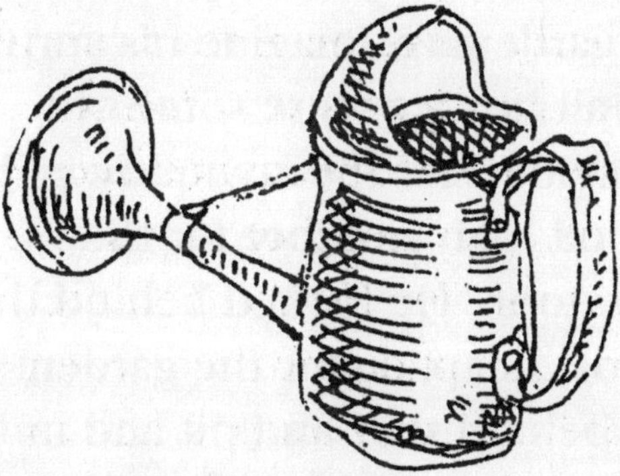

Jessica had seen him creeping up the stairs to Tim's bedroom with the garden tools. She guessed immediately what Sam was up to, and who was likely to get the blame. When Sam wasn't about, she spoke to Tim. The two of them whispered to each other for a few seconds and then smiled triumphantly.

Later that day, Sam and Tim's father went to the garden shed to do some gardening. Imagine his surprise when all he saw were some old flower pots and the lawnmower. He searched high and low for the garden tools. He looked behind the compost heap, under the garden steps, behind the sand pit and in the garage. But they weren't anywhere to be seen.

Then he started searching in the house. He looked in the kitchen cupboard, and was just looking under the stairs when something at the top of the stairs caught his eye. The handle from the garden spade was sticking out of the door to Sam's bedroom. Looking rather puzzled, he went upstairs and walked into Sam's bedroom. There, nestling neatly in the cupboard, were the rest of the tools.

"Sam, come up here immediately," called his father.

Sam, not realising anything was amiss, came sauntering upstairs. Suddenly he saw all the garden tools that he had so carefully hidden in Tim's cupboard now sitting in his cupboard. He was speechless.

"Right," said his father, "before you go out to play, you can take all the tools back down to the garden shed. Then you can cut the grass. Then you can dig over the flower beds, and then you can do the weeding."

Well, it took Sam hours to do all the gardening. Tim and Aunt Jessica watched from the window and clutched their sides with laughter. Sam never did find out how all the garden tools found their way into his bedroom, but I think you've guessed, haven't you?

Lucy and the Green Door

LUCY JENKINS lived in an ordinary house, in an ordinary street, in an ordinary town. At the back of Lucy's house was an ordinary garden with ordinary flowers and an ordinary path. But down the path at the bottom of the garden was a tree that was not ordinary at all! It was a huge old oak tree, and at the bottom of the tree was a very small green door, only just big enough for Lucy to squeeze through. This was Lucy's secret, because only she knew about the door. But what lay behind the door was Lucy's best secret of all!

Each afternoon Lucy would go down the garden path and knock lightly on the door. On the third knock the door would swing open wide, and the chief elf would be there to welcome her inside.

"Come inside, little Lucy," the elf would always say, "and have some tea."

Inside, Lucy would meet some very special friends indeed! First there were Penelope and Geraldine, two of the gentlest and sweetest fairies it was possible to imagine. Then there were Basil and Granville, who were rather mischievous imps (but who made Lucy laugh with their tricks and jokes), and there were the storytellers, who would sit for hours with Lucy and tell her the greatest tales from all the corners of the world. And of course there was the chief elf, who would make the most delicious milkshakes and scones with heaps of cream for Lucy to eat.

The world behind the green door was a wonderful place, and Lucy would always go home after-

wards feeling very cheerful and jolly. On one particular visit to the world behind the green door Lucy had just finished a scrumptious tea of cocoa and toasted marshmallows with the chief elf, when she went off to play games with Basil and Granville. They were playing blind man's buff, and Lucy roared with laughter as Basil sneaked up on the blindfolded Granville and tickled him in the ribs, making him squeal and beg for the teasing to stop.

Now just recently, Lucy had been feeling down in the dumps because very soon she would be going to school and would only be able to visit her friends at weekends.

But they assured her that they would never forget her, and that as long as she was always a true friend to them she could visit as often or as little as she liked. This cheered Lucy up considerably, and then they took her to visit the storytellers so that her happiness was complete. Of all the delights behind the green door, the storytellers were Lucy's favourite. They told her stories of how the whales had learned to sing, and of where the stars went when the sun had risen in the sky and they had slipped from view.

Because of the assurances of the fairies, Lucy was not too worried when the day finally came for her to join all the other boys and girls of her age at school. Every day, Lucy would go to school and then afterwards would visit her friends behind the green door. As winter came round and the days grew dark she only visited at weekends, and looked forward to the holidays when she could visit them every day once more.

Meanwhile, at school, Lucy had made friends with a girl called Jessica, and although she told Jessica

all about her family and her home, she didn't at first tell her about her extraordinary tree with the little green door and the magic world that lay beyond. Lucy did tell Jessica all the stories that she was told by the storytellers, however, and Jessica grew more and more curious about

where she had heard all the wonderful tales. Every day, Jessica would ask more and more questions, and Lucy found it more and more difficult to avoid telling her about her secret. Eventually, Lucy gave in and told Jessica all about her adventures behind the green door.

Jessica scoffed and laughed when Lucy told her about the chief elf, and Basil, Granville, Penelope and Geraldine. She howled with laughter at the thought of the wonderful teas and the stories that followed. Jessica thought that Lucy was making the whole thing up! When Lucy protested, and said it was true, Jessica told her that it simply wasn't possible — that there were no such things as elves and fairies and imps and strange and wonderful worlds behind doors in trees. Lucy was distraught, and decided to take Jessica to the green door.

On the way home Lucy started to worry. What if she really had imagined it all? But if her wonderful friends didn't exist, how could she possibly know them? Jessica walked beside Lucy, still teasing her and laughing about Lucy's 'invisible' friends!

When Lucy and Jessica reached the bottom of the garden, Lucy was about to tap lightly on the green door at the bottom of the oak tree when she suddenly noticed the door had disappeared. She rubbed her eyes and looked again, but it simply wasn't there!

Jessica smirked and laughed at Lucy, calling her silly and babyish to believe in magic and fairy tales, and then ran off back down the road to school. Lucy could not face going back to school that afternoon, and when her mother saw her enter the house she thought she must be ill — she looked so upset! Lucy went to bed early and cried herself to sleep.

And when Lucy slept she started to dream. The chief elf, Basil and Granville, Penelope and Geraldine and the storytellers were all there in the dream.

Then Penelope and Geraldine stepped forward and hugged Lucy, and the hug was so real that Lucy began to hope it wasn't a dream! Then they all hugged her and asked why she hadn't been to see them for so long, and why they had not been able to reach out to her except now in the deepest of sleeps. Lucy explained what had happened on her last visit, and told them all about Jessica, and then Geraldine spoke.

"Little Lucy," she said, "you are special. You believe in magic and you believe in the little people. And because you believe, you are able to see us and live among us. But those who don't believe will always be shut out from our world. You must keep your belief, little Lucy."

With a huge surge of happiness

Lucy woke up, dressed quickly and ran out of her ordinary house, down the ordinary path in the ordinary garden up to the extraordinary tree, and was delighted to see the green door once more! She knocked very lightly and, after the third tap, the door swung open to reveal the chief elf. "Come inside, little Lucy," the elf said happily, "and have some tea."

The Missing Scarf

KANGA WAS VERY proud of her stripy knitted scarf. She had made it herself and she had also made a smaller matching one for her son, Joey. Kanga used to hop through the bush with her scarf streaming out behind her, while Joey's could just be seen poking out of the top of her pouch. Now Joey was older, he was too big for Kanga's pouch, but he still wore his scarf as he hopped along beside his mother.

Then one day Kanga woke up to

find that her beautiful scarf was missing. She searched high and low but it was nowhere to be found. Eventually she decided that she would have to go out into the bush to look for it.

"Stay here," she said to Joey. "I'll try not to be long. I'm sure to find my scarf soon." Kanga hopped off into the bush and started to search among the roots of trees and under stones.

She had gone quite a long way when, looking up into the branches of a eucalyptus tree, she spotted Koala. Now Koala was usually to be found asleep, but this time she was busy preparing a meal of eucalyptus leaves for her children. Kanga looked up at Koala and then her jaw dropped. For Koala was quite clearly wearing Kanga's scarf around her tummy. Then, to Kanga's horror, she saw Koala use the end of the scarf to wipe the teacups! "Koala," Kanga called. "Whatever do you think you're doing?"

Koala stopped cleaning the teacups and looked down through the branches of the eucalyptus tree at Kanga. "I'm wiping my teacups with my apron," she replied sleepily, "and I'll thank you not to interfere!" And with that, she yawned and moved several branches further up the tree.

Poor Kanga felt very embarrassed. How could she have mistaken Koala's striped apron for her own scarf? She hopped away and carried on further into the bush. After a while she could hear Kookaburra's familiar laughing call nearby.

"I know," thought Kanga, "I'll ask her if she's seen my scarf. She'd be able to spot it easily from up in the sky." She followed the sound of Kookaburra's call until she came to the tree where she lived. She looked up and, sure enough, there was Kookaburra flying towards the tree. Kanga was about to call up when her jaw dropped again. For Kookaburra was quite clearly carrying

Kanga's scarf in her beak. "Kookaburra," Kanga called. "Whatever do you think you're doing?"

"I'm lining my nest," mumbled Kookaburra through a beakful of stripy feathers. "And I'll thank you not to interfere," she added more distinctly, for she had now reached the nest and was arranging the feathers carefully in place.

Poor Kanga felt even more embarrassed. How could she have mistaken the feathers for her own scarf? She hopped away and carried on further into the bush.

After a while she reached a wide open plain and there she saw Emu running past with his baby chicks on his back. As he rushed past, Kanga's jaw dropped yet again. For Emu quite clearly had Kanga's scarf tucked in among his chicks. "Emu," called Kanga. "Whatever do you think you're doing?"

"I'm taking my chicks to safety," said Emu, glancing up at the sky as he sped away. "And you'd be wise to do the same," he added. Then Kanga

realised that what she had thought was her rolled-up scarf were just the striped chicks on Emu's back.

Poor Kanga felt even more embarrassed. How could she have made such a mistake? Then she felt a few spots of rain on her nose and, looking up, saw a huge black cloud overhead. There was no time to lose — she must find shelter.

She made a dash for some trees at the edge of the plain and soon found herself by a stream. She wandered along beside the stream feeling cold, wet, tired and miserable. Finally, she lay down in the wet grass beside the stream and tried to get to sleep. She shivered with cold and wondered how Joey was and whether he was behaving himself. She so hoped he hadn't got into mischief.

Just then there was a tap on her shoulder and there stood Platypus. "I could hear you in my burrow over there," she said pointing towards a hole beside the stream just above the water. "I thought you might like this to keep you warm," she added.

"My scarf!" exclaimed Kanga.

"Oh, is that what it is? I'm ever so sorry," said Platypus. "I've been using it as a blanket for my babies. It's rather cold and damp in my burrow, you know," she added, rather forlornly.

"Where did you find it?" asked Kanga.

"It was stuck on some thorns and I know I shouldn't have taken it, but I just thought it would be so nice for keeping my young ones warm," blurted Platypus, and she started to sob.

"There now," said Kanga, "don't cry. You can keep the scarf. You need it more than me."

Platypus stopped crying and

looked overjoyed. "Thank you," she said.

"No, thank you," said Kanga. "I've learned a lesson, which is not to get upset over a scarf, for I've ended up falling out with my friends."

Kanga made her way back home, but it took a long time because she apologised to all her friends on the way. When she explained what had happened Emu, Kookaburra and Koala all forgave her, and by the time she reached home she was feeling much better. Joey was there to greet her. "What have you been up to while I was away?" she asked.

"I made you this," he said.

He handed her a scarf. It was a very funny-looking scarf, made out of twigs, grass and feathers, but Kanga loved it very much.

"This is much more special than my old scarf," she said. And she gave Joey an extra big hug.

The Red Daffodil

IT WAS SPRING TIME and all the daffodils were pushing their heads up towards the warmth of the sun. Slowly, their golden petals unfolded to let their yellow trumpets dance in the breeze. One particular field of daffodils was a blaze of gold like all the others — but right in the middle was a single splash of red. For there in the middle was a red daffodil.

From the moment she opened her petals, the red daffodil knew she was different from the other flowers. They sneered at her and whispered to each other. "What a strange, poor creature!" said one.

"She must envy our beautiful

golden colour," said another.

And indeed it was true. The red daffodil wished very much that she was like the others. Instead of being proud of her red petals, she was ashamed and hung her head low. "What's wrong with me?" she thought. "Why aren't there any other red daffodils in the field?"

Passers-by stopped to admire the field of beautiful daffodils. "What a wonderful sight!" they exclaimed. And the daffodils' heads swelled with pride and danced in the breeze all the more merrily.

Then someone spotted the red daffodil right in the middle of the field. "Look at that extraordinary flower!" the man shouted. Everyone peered into the centre of the field.

"You're right," said someone else, "there's a red daffodil in the middle." Soon a large crowd had gathered, all pointing and laughing at the red daffodil.

She could feel herself blushing even redder at the attention. "How I wish my petals would close up again," she said to herself in anguish. But try as she might, her fine red trumpet stood out for all to see.

Now, in the crowd of people gathered at the edge of the field was a little girl. People were pushing and shoving and she couldn't see anything at all. At last, her father lifted her high upon his shoulders so that she could see into the field.

"Oh!" exclaimed the little girl in

a very big voice. "So that's the red daffodil. I think it's really beautiful. What a lucky daffodil to be so different."

And do you know, other people heard what the little girl said and they began to whisper to each other, "Well, I must say, I actually thought myself it was rather pretty, you know." Before long, people were praising the daffodil's beauty and saying it must be a very special flower. The red daffodil heard what the crowd was saying. Now she was blushing with pride and held her head as high as all the other daffodils in the field.

The other daffodils were furious. "What a foolish crowd," said one indignantly. "We are the beautiful ones!" They turned their heads away from the red daffodil and ignored her. She began to feel unhappy again.

By now word had spread far and wide about the amazing red daffodil and people came from all over the land to see her. Soon, the king's daughter got to hear about the red daffodil. "I must see this for myself," said the princess. She set off with her servant and eventually they came to the field where the red daffodil grew. When the princess saw her, she clapped her hands with glee.

"The red daffodil is more beautiful than I ever imagined," she cried. Then she had an idea. "Please bring my pet dove," she said to her servant.

The man looked rather puzzled, but soon he returned with the bird. "As you know," said the princess to the servant, "I am to be married tomorrow and I would dearly love to have that red daffodil in my wedding bouquet."

The princess sent the dove into the middle of the field and it gently picked up the daffodil in its beak and brought her back to where the princess stood. The princess carried the daffodil back to the palace. She put the daffodil in a vase of water and there she stayed until the next day.

In the morning, the princess's servant took the red daffodil to the church. She could hear the bells and see all the guests assembling for the wedding ceremony. Then she saw the princess arrive in a coach driven by four white horses. How lovely the princess looked in her white gown and her head crowned with deep red roses.

As the servant reached the church door, the princess's lady-in-waiting stepped forward holding a huge bouquet of flowers into which she placed the red daffodil just as the flowers were handed to the princess. For a while, the red daffodil was overcome by the powerful scents of the other flowers in the bouquet, but when at last she looked around her she realised, with astonishment, that all of them were red. There were red daisies, red lilies, red carnations and red foxgloves. "Welcome," said one of the daisies, "you're one of us." And for the first time in her life, the red daffodil felt really at home.

After the wedding, the princess scattered the flowers from her bouquet among the flowers in her garden. Every spring, when she opened her petals, the red daffodil found she was surrounded by lots of other red flowers, and she lived happily in the garden for many, many years.

The Sad Clown

BONGO THE CLOWN had a bit of a problem. Clowns were supposed to be happy, funny, jolly people, but Bongo was a very sad clown. Nothing at all seemed to make him laugh.

Whenever the circus came to town people from all around flocked to the big top hoping for an exciting day out. They thrilled to the daring performance of the high-wire act, as the acrobats leaped from one swinging trapeze to the next. They enjoyed the jugglers, who tossed bright, sparkling balls into the air while standing on one leg. And the crowd delighted in seeing the beautiful white horses parading

around the circus ring with the bareback riders balancing on their backs. When the seals came on, there was always a big cheer from the crowd, for everyone loved them and could watch their clever antics for hours.

But the biggest favourite of the crowd, especially with all the children, was the clown. Dressed in his big baggy trousers he would enter the circus ring with his funny walk. Everyone laughed to see him. They laughed even more when they saw his big floppy hat with the revolving flower on it. Even his painted clown face made them laugh.

But when his act started, the crowd thought they would burst with laughter. First of all his bicycle fell apart as he tried to ride around the ring. Then he fell out of his motor car when the seat tipped up.

By the time he had accidentally poured cold water down his trousers and fallen into the custard-filled swimming pool, the crowd were almost crying with laughter.

But beneath all the makeup, Bongo the sad clown wasn't smiling at all. In fact, he saw nothing funny at all in bicycles that fell apart as you used them, or cars that tipped you out as you went along, or having cold water poured down your trousers, or even ending up face first in a swimming pool full of custard. He simply hadn't got a sense of humour.

All the other performers in the circus decided they would try and cheer the sad clown up.

"I know," said the high-wire trapeze acrobat, "let's paint an even funnier face on him. That'll make him laugh."

So that's what they did, but Bongo still didn't laugh and was still just as sad.

"Let us perform some of our tricks, just for him," said the seals.

So they sat on their stools and tossed their big coloured balls to each other, clapped their flippers together and made lots of honking sounds. But Bongo still didn't laugh. In fact, nothing that anyone tried made poor Bongo smile. He was still a very sad clown.

Then Percival the ring master spoke. "You know, I think I know what the problem is," he said. "There is nothing a clown likes better than playing tricks on other clowns.

Perhaps if we had a second clown, that would cheer Bongo up."

So right away they hired another clown, called Piffle.

The circus arrived in the next town and soon it was time for Bongo and Piffle's act. Piffle started riding around on his bike while Bongo pretended to wash the car by throwing a bucket of water over it. Instead of the water landing on the car, of course, it went all over Piffle, who just happened to be cycling past at that moment. A little smile flickered across Bongo's face at the sight of the soaking wet Piffle.

Next, Bongo and Piffle pretended to be cooking, and Bongo

tripped while carrying two huge custard pics. Both landed right in Piffle's face. Bongo let out a huge chuckle of laughter when he saw Piffle's custard-covered face.

At the end of their act, the clowns were pretending to be decorators, painting up a ladder. Of course, you've guessed it. The ladders fell down and all the pots of paint landed on the two clowns. Bongo looked across at Piffle, who had a big paint pot stuck on his head, with paint dripping down his body. Bongo threw back his head and roared with laughter. Piffle thought Bongo looked just as funny with paint all over his body, too. And as for the crowd — well, they thought two clowns were even funnier than one and they clapped and cheered and filled the big top with laughter. After that Bongo was never a sad clown again.

Spooky Wood

Written by Angela Holroyd

IT WAS MR. OWL'S BIRTHDAY. The woodland animals were sitting in Steffy Squirrel's front room talking about the birthday party they were holding that night.

As usual, Maggie Magpie did most of the talking. In fact, it was hard to get her to stop.

"I bet I've got the *best* birthday present for Mr. Owl," she boasted, puffing up her feathers proudly. "It's a real brass ring, which will make a wonderful door knocker."

Poor Steffy Squirrel felt quite upset. She had been so busy

arranging the food for the party that she had completely forgotten about a present.

"I know where there's a lovely present," said Jessie Jay. "It's a beautiful red scarf and would suit Mr. Owl to perfection."

"Where? Tell me where!" said Steffy.

"Draped over a bush in ... in Moleland."

"MOLELAND!" all the animals shrieked out loud. For Moleland was the name that they had given to a spooky area deep in the heart of the wood. None of the animals would go near it — apart from the moles.

"Those bloomin' moles aren't to

be trusted," screeched Maggie Magpie. "If you ask me, the ghosts invited them to live in Spooky Wood, to help them play their nasty tricks on us."

"I've heard they leave messages for the spirits," chipped in Jessie Jay. "Mounds of earth piled high — secret signs that's what they are. Why, the earth itself trembles before a mole appears."

"Stuff and nonsense!" snapped Steffy Squirrel. "I've yet to meet someone who's actually met a ghost!"

"All right! All right Miss Know-it-all!" screamed Maggie Magpie. "If you think you know better than all of us, why don't you prove it? Go and fetch the red scarf from Spooky Wood. If you get back safely then we might stop believing in ghosts!" With this she puffed herself up even more and flew out of the window, squawking as she left.

"Visit Moleland — if you dare!"

After the other animals had gone, Steffy sat quietly thinking. The more she thought about the red scarf, the more she wanted it for Mr. Owl.

"I'll show them!" she said pulling on her coat and bonnet. Once out in the wood, she darted along quickly. But the farther she travelled, the thicker and darker the wood became.

The light from the moon cast spooky shadows. What was more, Steffy suddenly realized that she was lost. What a fool she had been not to listen to the others. Just then, a moonbeam lit up a tiny green door at the bottom of a grassy bank. She would never have noticed it had its little brass handle not caught the moonlight.

"Thank goodness!" said Steffy. "I'm sure whoever lives here will help me find my way home." But before she could clamber down the bank, an eerie howling noise filled the wood. "So the stories of ghosts are true," thought Steffy as the earth at her very feet started to move, rising upward into a huge mound. Too frightened to move, Steffy watched in amazement as a small pink nose appeared from the top of the mound, followed by a dark furry head. It wasn't a ghost at all — it was a mole!

"Goodness me, goodness me!" said Marmaduke Mole adjusting his thick glasses. "You look as if you've just seen a ghost, young squirrel. Did my noise frighten you?" he said, shaking the earth from a shiny silver trumpet. "I always sound a warning note on this before I surface, just in case anyone's standing up above. Wouldn't want to give them a shock now, would I?"

Steffy Squirrel began to laugh. How silly all the woodland animals had been — making up all those stories about spooks and spirits.

Marmaduke thought it was funny too.

"I have lived here for five years," he said, leading Steffy into his cozy home, "and I've never seen even a wisp of a ghost!"

Marmaduke Mole turned out to be very kind. He sat Steffy down to warm before a blazing log fire and gave her a delicious mug of nut broth.

She told him all about the party and the red scarf, how Maggie Magpie had dared her to venture into Spooky Wood, and what Jessie Jay had said.

"We moles cannot see very well in the daylight," explained Marmaduke. "So we don't often come up above ground. I'm sorry your friends are so frightened of us and our home."

"Well, I'm not," said Steffy smiling. "I will enjoy telling them the truth about Moleland."

"I will take you back to the party along the underground tunnels," said Marmaduke, when they had finished their broth. "There are definitely no ghouls down there!" And with that he wandered off and returned holding a lantern and a blue silk scarf.

"Do you think this would suit Mr. Owl?" he asked. Steffy was delighted. Before they left, Marmaduke collected his silver trumpet and a white sheet.

"I have an idea for these," he whispered mysteriously, but would say no more.

The pair set off along the dimly lit tunnels, with Marmaduke leading the way. Occasionally they met other underground travellers, including a family of beetles scuttling along with their tiny lanterns shining brightly in the darkness.

Steffy was surprised at how many windows and doors there were. She had counted over fifty by the time they reached the clearing where Mr. Owl's birthday party was being held. The tunnel ended at the bottom of a large tree. When Steffy popped out her head, she could see all her friends and neighbours gathered around a big table. The food was spread out and the musicians had arrived. The party was obviously about to begin.

Steffy was about to join them when Marmaduke whispered his secret plan in her ear. Then he put the trumpet to his lips and a loud haunting sound blasted out from the bottom of the tree.

All the woodland animals and birds looked at one another in amazement as a ghostly voice boomed out:

"Beware the ghoul from Spooky Wood
From Moleland he has come.
His face is covered with a hood,
He's come to join the fun!"

With that, Marmaduke loomed out of the tree covered in the white sheet.

"It's a ggg. . .ghost!" screamed Maggie Magpie. But before she could fly away, Steffy stepped into the clearing.

"That's where you're wrong," Steffy Squirrel said laughing. "This is what you've all been frightened of!" And she pulled off the sheet just as Marmaduke gave another blast on his trumpet. Steffy burst out laughing, and, soon, so did everyone else. Everyone that is, except Maggie Magpie. She was sulking at the top of a tree and refused to come down.

"You need never be frightened of Spooky Wood again," explained Steffy Squirrel as the band struck up a jolly tune. "Marmaduke is the only 'ghost' you're ever likely to find there!"

And so the birthday party began. All the animals made Marmaduke very welcome, especially Mr. Owl, who was thrilled with his birthday present. In fact, it was even better than the brass ring!

The Ghost Train

Written by Andrew Charman

PAGAN PLACE was a tall, dark house that stood on a hill at the edge of town. It could be seen for miles around and all the people of the town were scared of going near it.

Sam's grandmother said that when she was young, an old woman by the name of Mrs Crablook had lived there. She wore long black dresses in the style of a hundred years before, she never went out, and everyone, even the grown-ups, was frightened of her. After the old lady's death, the house had been put up for sale. But no one came to look at it; no one dared to.

Over the years, Pagan Place fell

slowly into a state of decay. The hinges on the doors rusted solid, the brickwork crumbled, and all you could see through the windows was a cloud of cobwebs. The yard was choked with weeds, and the trees had become scraggly and twisted with age. Bats made their home in the roof, and they could be seen circling around the chimneys at dusk. People who were brave enough to pass by the house at night said that they had heard strange noises coming from inside, and some even reported seeing faces at the windows.

When Sam, Billy, and Clara were outside in the street, they were always aware of Pagan Place. In the dark shadows of evening, the house seemed to grow and lean menacingly towards the town.

Billy's grandmother was always telling them that Pagan Place was haunted. But although they thought the house was spooky, not one of them really believed that ghosts lived there. Little did they know!

Inside the gloomy old house, at the end of the darkest passage you could ever imagine, there stood a door. It was shrouded by cobwebs and never opened. Behind it was a room full of old furniture. The curtains hung in tatters at the windows and a thick layer of dust covered every object. Anyone entering this dark and dusty place on a sunny, autumn afternoon would have been surprised to hear the sound of a piano playing faintly somewhere in the stillness.

They would have been even more surprised to see a tall, unhappy-looking man standing in front of the room's gilded mirror. He was dressed in a black suit, with an old-fashioned wing-collar, and huge brown shoes. Taking a deep breath, he pulled his face into a grisly grimace and moaned:

"OOOOoooooohhhhhh!"

"Oh, come on, Herbert," said another man who was lounging on the moth-eaten sofa, dressed as a pirate captain. "You've been dead for fifty years. Surely you can look more scary than that?"

"Well, I'm sorry," replied Herbert in a gloomy voice. "I don't feel well and I'm out of practice. I'm doing my best."

"Look, watch me!" said the other

ghost, and he leapt up, let out a blood-chilling scream and pulled off his head. Then he tucked it under his arm and danced around the room. "See! It's easy!" he laughed.

Just then the ghost who had been playing the piano stepped forward and said in a very wellspoken voice:

"The problem, my dears, is that we don't have anyone to scare. It's all very well pulling faces in front of mirrors. What we need is real, living people to frighten." The others nodded.

Mr Fergusson was well-respected among the other ghosts. He had been dead for over 400 years. He wore very old-fashioned clothes and had once had dinner with William Shakespeare. He turned to Mrs Crablook.

"What do you think, Madam?"

The old lady was busy knitting cobwebs in a dark corner. She made them for the spiders who were too old to make their own.

"I think we need to launch a campaign of terror," she said. "We're wasting our time in this house. No one comes here. We must leave the house and scare the wits out of the people in this town before we all forget how to do it."

With that, the old lady reached over and pulled a rope that hung by her side. The rope fell from the ceiling in a cloud of dust, bringing bits of plaster down with it. Deep in the recesses of the house, a bell rang. A moment later, in floated Clarence the spirit, balancing a tray of tea things on one arm. Clarence was pale and wispy, a shapeless creature who flew everywhere.

"Over here," called Mrs Crablook. "Yes... er... thank you Clarence."

Clarence flew around the room, his cloud-like body curling around the ornaments and picture frames. The others tried to steady him, but he was out of control again. He floated up to the ceiling, circled three times around the light-fitting, and disappeared.

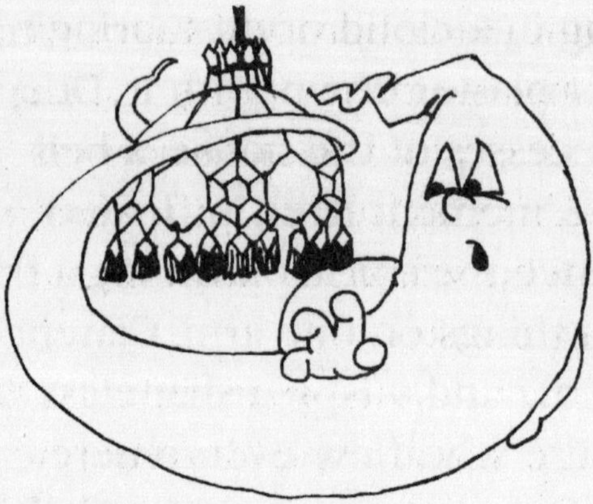

"Oh, dear," sighed Mrs Crablook. "Will someone please catch up with Clarence and fetch the tea things?"

Down at the bottom of the hill, the townspeople were preparing for Halloween, the night when ghosts haunt the living and witches fly through the sky. Everyone was planning to dress up in a Halloween costume. Sam, Billy, and Clara were busy making their outfits and they were all excited. Sam put on his monster mask and crept up behind Clara who was busy finishing off her witch's cloak.

"Grrrrggghh," roared Sam. Clara let out a scream and clutched her heart.

"If you do that once more," she shouted, putting on her tall, black hat and waving her wand at her brother, "I'll turn you into a frog." Sam hopped out of the room laughing and Clara followed, cackling behind him. But they both stopped suddenly in the hall and froze in horror at the sight of a pale, shapeless figure before them...

The spirit turned and raised its arms and moaned. They recognized the voice — it was Billy!

Throughout the town, excitement was growing. Witches cackled and whizzed here and there on broomsticks, monsters clomped and groaned up and down the street, and spectres floated in and out of rooms. The next day was Halloween when there would be a street parade, a giant funfair, and a bonfire party.

The children were planning to be more scary than ever before. Sam, Billy, and Clara tried their disguises out on the family. Their grandmother was not impressed — she'd seen too many ghosts to be frightened of children in costumes. But Uncle Tom was so scared that he let go of his lawn mower which careered straight into the neighbour's pond. Their mother screamed and stepped back into the dog's food bowl, and Mrs Coleman from next door put her hands to her face, ran inside, and wasn't seen until the following Wednesday.

At Pagan Place, preparations were also underway. Mrs Crablook draped cobwebs over her ancient clothes. Herbert practised his menacing faces and Clarence drifted through the eerie house making things go bump. In his room, the Captain pulled off his head and put it back on again several times until the action was quite smooth and unlikely to go wrong.

Meanwhile, Mr Fergusson found some spiders who were happy to live in his beard and busied himself by pressing his clothes. Soon, the ghostly group was ready to give the town the fright of its life. They had no idea that they had chosen to do their spooking on the night of Halloween!

The night started well. A storm raged through the district accompanied by terrible thunder and long, forked fingers of lightning. Owls hooted somewhere in the darkness of the woods and spiders busily wove webs where there had never been webs before. The ghosts of Pagan Place floated noiselessly through the doors and walls of their crumbling home and made for the town.

"I think we should spook this one first," said Mrs Crablook, pointing to one of the nearby houses.

Everyone nodded, and the Captain's head fell off. Herbert stood at the front door and knocked loudly and slowly three times.

Clarence floated up to a bedroom window and peered in, while Mrs Crablook scratched her long fingernails against the downstairs windows.

Inside, the McTavish twins were expecting their friends to arrive at any moment. They were already wearing their Halloween costumes. Bob looked grisly as a green and yellow ghoul with huge boils on his neck. Geraldine wore a wig of rubber snakes that flopped and curled around her forehead.

"That will be the others," said Geraldine when she heard the knock at the door. "Come on, Bob! Let's give them a scare."

The two children flung open the door. Bob roared and dribbled from the corner of his mouth, and Geraldine shook her head and made the snakes wriggle and writhe.

Herbert had never seen anything so frightening, not in life or death.

"H... H... Help!" he stammered, and he turned and fled. He ran past Mrs Crablook who was staring in horror at the monstrous creatures in the doorway. Mr Fergusson and the Captain were already heading for the street, running as fast as they could.

"Quick! Follow Herbert!" they shouted.

The twins were pleased with themselves.

"Wow!" said Bob. "We really scared them!"

"I've never seen Sam and Billy run so fast," laughed Geraldine. "Clara's costume looked great, didn't it?"

As they turned back into the house, Bob and Geraldine met Clarence in the hallway. Clarence floated up to the ceiling and moaned, "OOoooohhh." Then he took one look at Bob, who at that moment was struggling to get out of

his mask, gulped and sped through a wall.

"Bob, that was a real ghost," said Geraldine, excitedly. "It went through the wall!"

But Bob hadn't seen Clarence — he had been too busy trying to free himself from his mask.

"Nonsense," he said. "There's no such thing as a real ghost."

The inhabitants of Pagan Place were a long way from their home by now and in a state of great confusion. They ran down the main street of the town in utter horror. Everywhere they turned they saw ghosts, ghouls, monsters, and witches. At one point, a demon with a forked tail and horns came up to the Captain and shook his hand. The Captain's hand came away at the wrist.

"Brilliant!" cried the demon appreciatively. "How do you do that?" The Captain didn't wait to answer — he picked up his hand and ran.

The ghosts were just passing the entrance to the funfair when Sam, Billy, and Clara appeared out of an alleyway in their Halloween costumes.

"L... L... Look!" stammered Herbert. "More of them." And, without looking where they were going, the ghosts blundered into the fairground to escape.

"Hey, wait for us," shouted Sam after the ghosts, and then turning to the others he said: "Come on, there must be something happening at the funfair. *Be scary!*" So Clara and Billy followed Sam, laughing all the way. Up ahead, Herbert was paler than he'd ever been before, Mrs Crablook had lost most of her cobwebs, and Mr Fergusson, usually so smartly dressed, was looking shabby and red in the face.

"Quick! On the Ghost Train," cried Clarence, spotting a sign. "Perhaps we'll shake them off there." The ghosts passed through the walls of the Ghost Station and climbed on board the waiting train. It was silent inside. Then they heard a clacking sound.

"SSssshhh," said Mr Fergusson. "What's that noise?"

"It's m... m... my teeth," stammered Herbert. "I've never b... b... been on a g... ghost train before. I'm scared." And he took out his teeth and put them in his pocket to stop them chattering. Suddenly, the train gave a lurch, then a jolt, and started rolling forward.

"Hold on everyone," shouted Mr Fergusson.

The Ghost Train gathered speed and disappeared into the darkness of a tunnel. Suddenly, lights flashed and lit up ghoulish faces that leered and grinned out of the shadows. A bright, white skeleton leapt out of nowhere and dangled in front of them. Something wet hit Herbert in his left ear and a mechanical spider fell from the ceiling. The darkness was filled with the sounds of groaning, moaning, creaking, and eerie laughing. Eventually, the train slowed down

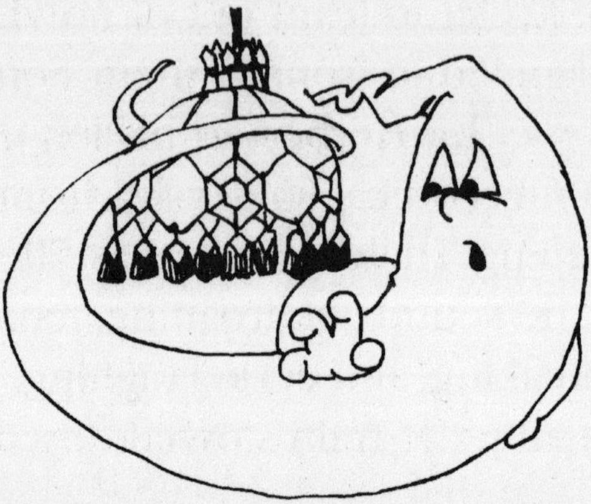

and stopped. Mrs Crablook looked at Mr Fergusson with surprise.

"Well, that wasn't very scary, was it?" she said.

"Did you see that spectre?" asked Clarence. "It was rubbish. I could do better than that any day."

"I wasn't frightened either," said Herbert, opening his eyes for the first time.

Just then the ghosts heard the sound of voices and the train wobbled as people climbed on board.

"Oh, no!" cried Clarence. "It's those monsters again. Whatever shall we do?"

"But look!" cried Mr Fergusson, staring hard at the nearest passenger. "They're not monsters at all. They're children wearing silly costumes — and that has given me a *brilliant* idea!" Quickly, he whispered a plan to the others. They knew exactly what he had in mind.

The Captain unfastened the cardboard skeleton and stood in its place. Mrs Crablook sat in a rocking chair beside the rails and Mr Fergusson stood where the lights would shine directly onto his elegant face.

The children on the Ghost Train had never had a better ride. They whooped and hollered and screamed as the train flashed through the darkness. They were terrified when they saw Mrs Crablook in her rocking chair scowling at them. The Captain horrified everyone by removing his head and spinning it on his finger as if it were a basketball. Clarence followed the train throughout, swooping in and out of the carriages. But the best performance was Herbert's. He stood in the middle of the tracks as the train approached.

All the passengers held their breath and waited for him to step out of the way. But he didn't.

The Captain stepped onto the tracks as well. The train roared straight through him and, as it sped away, he turned and waved at the passengers. When the children arrived back at the platform, they were laughing and cheering.

"That's the best ghost train ever," laughed Sam.

"And you could see right through

that old lady. It was amazing!" said Billy.

"It was as if they were real ghosts," said Clara, excitedly. "Come on, let's go round again."

So they went round again, and again, and again until they were exhausted. The ghosts perfected their act. They had never been so scary, nor had so much fun. So they decided to stay for a little while.

"We can always go home again when it gets boring," suggested Mrs Crablook.

Over the months that followed, the Ghost Train became famous for miles around. Everyday, the carriages were packed with people who wanted to be scared out of their wits. They were never disappointed. People who came again and again were surprised to find that the ride never seemed to be the same twice. The man who ran the Ghost Train kept it open all year round and made so much money that he eventually bought Pagan Place. For some reason it wasn't scary any more.

The ghosts heard about it one day, after a good spooking. But instead of being upset Mrs Crablook smiled at the others and said:

"You know, I don't think I want to go home after all. I'm just getting into the spirit of the thing!"

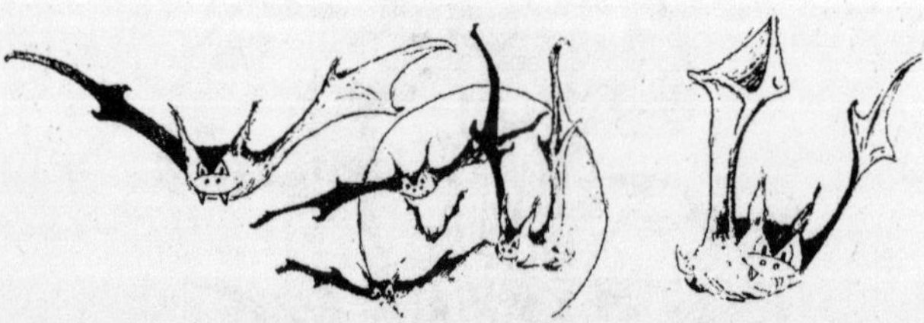

The Sad Snowman

Written by Angela Holroyd

IT WAS CHRISTMAS EVE. All the children in the village were very excited because it had snowed during the night, and they had decided to build a snowman.

"I want to build one as big as a house," said Izzy, the little sister of Jim and Jenny.

That's exactly what all the children did. With red noses and numb fingers, they worked all through the afternoon, watched in amusement by the ducks on a nearby pond. Buckeye — one of four cats that lived with old Mrs. Tumpy at the edge of the village — also watched the goings-on with great interest. What were the children building?

At last, the snow statue was finished. The children cheered loudly when Jim, who was tallest, put the final touches to the snowman's face. He used pieces of coal for the eyes, a carrot for a nose, and put his own hat on top of the snowman's head.

"He almost looks as if he could talk," said Izzy, looking at the snowman over her shoulder as they trudged home for supper.

Soon the snowman stood alone in the twilight. Even the ducks had tucked themselves in for the night. Buckeye had disappeared to find his three friends — Keaki, Hickory, and Kansan — so they too could see the massive snow figure. All four cats gazed up at him in wonder.

"He looks a bit frightening," whispered Keaki to the others. To their amazement they heard a heavy, sad sigh and an icy tear rolled down the snowman's face.

"I don't mean to look fierce," the snowman sniffed. "But it's not something I can do anything about. I'm bound to look this way, because I haven't got a heart."

"How do you know?" asked Hickory, who didn't seem in the least surprised that the snowman could talk.

"Because not one of the children — not even little Izzy — said that they loved me," said the sad snow-man. "And according to snowman legend, you must be told that you are loved before you can have a heart.

"You see, when a snowman melts, the icy water flows into

streams, rivers, and down to the sea if he has a heart — he lives forever as a part of nature. With no heart I will simply melt into nothing. I will just disappear!" And with that another enormous tear rolled down his cheek.

The cats felt very sorry for the snowman.

"What if *we* said we loved you?" asked Kansan who was very kind-hearted.

"That's very nice of you, but I don't think it would work," said the snowman with another sigh. "You see, it has to be said by a child."

For a while there was silence, then Kansan spoke up softly.

"You're not the only one that's sad," she said. "We're all pretty miserable today, too. Mrs. Tumpy is coming out of hospital tomorrow and it's Christmas day..."

"And we haven't got a present for her," chipped in Buckeye.

The snowman thought about this for a moment, then suddenly an idea came to him.

"We must go to the Kingdom of Ice!" he said. "Every year on Christmas Eve Father Christmas stops off there on his way back to the North Pole after delivering all his Christmas presents. He might have a present left over for Mrs. Tumpy."

"But the Kingdom of Ice must

be a long way from here!" exclaimed Hickory. "Even if Father Christmas does have a spare present, I can't see how we are all going to get there?"

The snowman smiled kindly and winked.

"Tonight is a very special night," he said. "On Christmas Eve all kinds of magic can happen." And with that he lifted up his large, white arms and softly breathed a magic message into the night air.

Buckeye, Hickory, Keaki, and Kansan all stared hard at the moonlit sky. One of the clouds seemed to be floating closer and closer until it gently came to rest in front of them. It was a snowcloud sleigh, and it was being pulled by a reindeer. The sleigh was as soft as a cloud and as whitc as snow, and within seconds all five of them had climbed on board.

At a word from the snowman the sleigh rose up into the air. And in no time at all the rooftops and trees of the village were far below them. All that surrounded them was the

vast, inky sky and the twinkling of a thousand tiny stars.

Before long, the cats spotted twinkling blue lights in the distance. Gliding closer, they saw that the lights were shining from hundreds of icicle towers which sparkled in the darkness.

As the sleigh glided gently to the ground, snowpeople of all shapes and sizes came to meet them. In the middle stood Jack Frost who led them to the Ice Palace where, seated on a frozen throne, sat the Snowflake Queen.

"Welcome to the Kingdom of Ice," she said in a silvery voice. "How can we help you?"

Hickory explained that they were looking for a present for Mrs. Tumpy and that they hoped Father Christmas might help them. Father Christmas was sent for immediately, but he had just given his very last present away to the Palace cook.

"Tell me what the old woman loves more than anything else in the world," said the Queen.

"That's easy!" piped up Keaki. "She adores trees."

"Then I think I may be able to help you," smiled the Queen. She sent for the Ice Palace gardener and whispered something in his ear. He scurried away and came back very shortly carrying the most beautiful tree the cats had ever seen. It was made entirely of delicate, lacy snowflakes. The Queen handed it to Hickory.

"This tree will bloom throughout the winter," she said, "and will bring your owner health and happiness." Then she turned to the snowman, who was still looking a little sad.

"There seems to be something troubling you Mr. Snowman," she said kindly. "Tell me about it if you will. Maybe I can help you too."

So in a sad voice the snowman told the story of the snowman legend and how, without a heart, he would melt and disappear forever when Spring came. When he had finished his story, the Snowflake

Queen smiled sweetly and took his snowy hand in hers.

"Of course you have a heart," she said. "What you heard is only an old legend. Look what you have done tonight — without a heart you would never have wanted to help your new friends. Only someone with a heart cares for others."

The night sky was beginning to lighten. Soon it would be daylight. It was time for the five visitors to

return to the village. The snowcloud sleigh awaited them outside. Carrying the snowflake tree between them, the four cats climbed aboard. The Queen escorted the snowman, holding in her hand a mysterious parcel. Just as the snowman was about to climb into the sleigh she undid the paper to reveal a large, red, heart-shaped badge.

"This is to remind you that when the thaw comes and the snow melts you have nothing to worry about," she whispered and pinned the heart carefully to his chest.

The next morning all the village children gathered on the green to show each other the presents that

Father Christmas had brought them. It was Izzy who first noticed the snowman.

"Look Jim," she cried excitedly to her brother. "Our snowman has had a present too. I wonder where he got it from?"

"Perhaps it was father Christmas," answered Jim jokingly.

The snowman had to hide a grin. Only Buckeye, Hickory, Keaki and Kanson knew what had really happened.

The Toys That Ran Away

"PUT YOUR toys away, Lucy," said Lucy's mother from the kitchen, "it's time to get ready for bed." Lucy gave a great big sigh.

"Do I really have to?" she asked, knowing full well what the answer was going to be.

"Yes, of course you do," said her mother. "You shouldn't have to be told each time to put your toys away. You really don't look after them properly."

It was true. Lucy never had been very good at looking after her toys. Once she left her beautiful new doll outside in her pram and she had become ruined after it rained. Then she had carelessly dropped her tea set on the floor and some of the cups had broken. And she was forever just pushing all her toys back in the cupboard in a hurry, instead of putting them away carefully. Worse still, when she was in a temper, she would throw her toys, and sometimes she would even kick them.

Tonight Lucy was in another of her 'can't be bothered' moods. She grabbed a handful of toys and threw them into the cupboard. In first went some dolls, which all landed on their heads and then fell in a heap. Next Lucy threw in the little tables and chairs from the doll's house. They landed with a bounce and came to a stop in the corner. Without even looking behind her, Lucy then picked up some puzzles and a skipping rope, and tossed them into the cupboard, too. They landed with a crash on the floor of the cupboard as well.

"That's that," said Lucy. She closed the cupboard door, squashing the toys even more, and went into the bathroom to have her bath.

Inside the toy cupboard Teddy, one of the toys, spoke. "I'm not going to stay here a moment longer," he said.

"Nor me," said Katie the ragdoll.

"If we aren't going to be loved, we aren't staying either," chimed the doll's house furniture.

"I want to be somewhere where I'm not thrown around," said one of the puzzles.

"So do we," said the roller blades.

One after another, all the toys

agreed that they weren't going to stay. They decided they would all go back to Toyland and wait to be given to some children who would love them more.

The next morning, Lucy decided that she would play with her skipping rope. When she opened the toy cupboard, she couldn't believe her eyes. All the toys had vanished. The shelves were completely empty.

At first Lucy thought her mother had moved them, but her mother said she hadn't.

"I expect you've put them somewhere yourself, Lucy, and can't remember where you've left them," said her mother, not very helpfully.

All day, Lucy searched high and low for her missing toys, but they were nowhere to be found. She went to bed in tears that night, wondering if she would ever be able to play with her toys again. She was already missing them terribly.

That night, Lucy was suddenly woken by a noise in her bedroom. Was she seeing things or was that a little fairy at the bottom of her bed? "Who are you?" asked Lucy.

"I am the special messenger from Toyland," replied the fairy. "I have been sent to tell you that all your toys have run away back to Toyland, because you treated them badly."

"Oh, I do miss my toys so much," cried Lucy.

"Well, if you really do, then you had better come and tell them yourself," said the fairy.

With that, the fairy floated over to Lucy and took her hand. The fairy then beat her wings so fast that they became a blur. At the same time Lucy felt herself being lifted from her bed. Out of Lucy's bedroom window they both flew, across fields and forests, until it became too misty for Lucy to see anything at all.

Suddenly, they were floating down to the ground. The mist lifted, and Lucy found herself in the grounds of a huge fairy-tale castle with tall, pointed turrets and warm, yellow lights twinkling from the windows.

"This is Toyland Castle," exclaimed the fairy, as she led Lucy to a large red door.

The fairy knocked on the door. "Do enter, please," said a voice.

Lucy found herself in a large, cosy room with a huge log fire.

Sitting in the corner was a kindly looking little man wearing a carpenter's apron and holding a broken wooden doll. "Hello," he said, "you've come to ask your toys to return, haven't you?"

"Well... er... yes," said Lucy, not really quite knowing what to say.

"It's up to them to decide, of course," said the little man. "They only come back here if they are mistreated. If they are broken, I repair them, and then they go to other children who love them more."

"But I do love my toys," wept Lucy.

"Then come and tell them yourself," smiled the little man.

He led Lucy into another room, and there, to her surprise, were all her toys. Not only that, but they were all shiny and new again. Nothing was broken or chipped or scratched. Lucy ran up to her toys.

"Please, toys, please come home again. I really do love you and miss you, and I promise I shall never mistreat you again," she cried. She picked up Teddy and gave him a big hug. Then she did the same thing to all the other toys.

"Well, it's up to the toys now," said the little man. "You must go back home again with the fairy messenger and hope that they will give you another chance."

With that, the fairy messenger took Lucy's hand, and soon they were floating over her own garden again and through her bedroom window. Lucy was so tired she didn't

even remember falling asleep when she got into bed.

In the morning she awoke, still rather sleepy, and rushed to the toy cupboard. There, neatly lined up on the shelves, were all her toys. Lucy was overjoyed. From that day on, she always treated her toys well and took great care of them.

Lucy never was quite sure whether the whole thing was a dream or not, but it certainly did the trick whatever it was.

There was one thing that really puzzled her though.

If it had just been a dream, why were all the toys so shiny and new again?